GET CODING
WITH LOGIC

Why is understanding logic useful? Find out with fun puzzles and games!

Kevin Wood

WINDMILL BOOKS

New York

Published in 2018 by **Windmill Books**, An Imprint of Rosen Publishing
29 East 21st Street, New York, NY 10010

Produced for Windmill Books by Alix Wood Books
Designed by Alix Wood
Editor: Eloise Macgregor
Editor for Gareth Stevens: Kerri O'Donnell

Photo credits: Cover background © Shutterstock; All robot artwork © Adobe Stock Images and Alix Wood;
all other art © Alix Wood

CATALOGING-IN-PUBLICATION DATA

Names: Wood, Kevin.
Title: Get coding with logic / Kevin Wood.
Description: New York : Windmill Books, 2018. | Series: Computer-free coding | Includes index.
Identifiers: ISBN 9781499482584 (pbk.) | ISBN 9781499484182 (library bound) | ISBN 9781499482478 (6 pack)
Subjects: LCSH: Computer programming--Juvenile literature. | Programming languages (Electronic computers)--
    Juvenile literature. | Computers--Juvenile literature.
Classification: LCC QA76.52 W66 2018 | DDC 005--dc23

Printed in the United States of America
CPSIA compliance information: Batch # BS17WM: For further information contact Gareth Stevens, New York, New York at 1-800-542-2595.

Contents

Coding and Logic

Logic is reasoning. If someone is using logic in everyday life, they are explaining something by following a set of rules. Guessing is not using logic. Everything that a computer does involves logic. A computer cannot guess or be **random**. At its most basic level, a computer can only test to see if something is true or false.

TRUE

FALSE

TRUE OR FALSE?

Computers use a number system known as **binary**. The binary number system uses two numbers, 0 and 1. Computers only really understand two things — their electrical supply being off, or on. Coders can use these two states to get the computer to test for True or False, Yes or No, or On or Off.

CODING TIPS

When coders **program** computers, the computer language they use changes the commands into binary. Coders don't have to know binary, but it is helpful to understand the logic behind the two states (off or on).

There's a joke that says "Binary is as easy as 1, 10, 11." Read the next page and see if you can decode the joke!

GETTING BINARY

Binary is actually simple to learn. Look at the chart below. If any numbers have a 1 under them, you add those numbers together. Here, there is 1 under 4 and 1.

64	32	16	8	4	2	1
0	0	0	0	1	0	1

4 plus 1 is 5.
So, 5 in binary is written

0 0 0 0 1 0 1

Can you work out what these binary numbers are, using this shorter chart?

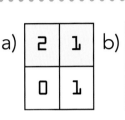

a)
2	1
0	1

b)
2	1
1	0

c)
2	1
1	1

Answers are on page 32

GET Programming

How does a computer use True or False to work out logical solutions? Coders get the computer to ask a question. The answer to that question can only be True or False.

You have some hens and you want to put their eggs into boxes. Each egg box holds six eggs. If you have more than six eggs, you need a second egg box.

Question:
    Have I got more than six eggs?
Answer:
    I have seven eggs — True [get another box]
    I have three eggs — False [don't get another box]

Can you think of some questions you could ask that would only need True or False answers?

Following Instructions

A computer can only do what it is told to do. Code is how we to tell the computer to do things. Coders write a set of instructions, known as an **algorithm**. The computer is then asked to perform the algorithm.

What does an algorithm look like?

An algorithm is just a simple step-by-step list that shows how to do something.

FEEDING THE DOG

It is important that an algorithm's steps are in the right order. Can you see what is wrong with the order of the code below? Can you sort the instructions into the correct order?

1. Get can
2. Get can opener
3. Open can
4. Spoon out dog food on kitchen floor
5. Put bowl on kitchen floor

Answers are on page 32

GET Programming

How good are you at writing clear instructions? Try to play this game with a friend. Make an obstacle course on the floor using cushions. Now imagine your friend is a computer-powered robot. Write an algorithm telling them how to walk from one end of the course to the other without touching a cushion. Use **precise** instructions such as "Walk two paces forward. Walk one step left." Your friend must follow your instructions EXACTLY. They mustn't try to guess what you meant. If they touch a cushion, add a point to your score.

Walk two paces forward.
Walk one step left.
Walk two paces forward.
Walk one step right.
Walk two paces forward.

Take turns writing the algorithm and being the robot. The one with the least points at the end wins!

The algorithm you wrote to program the robot around the obstacle course on page 7 probably only works for that particular obstacle course. If you moved the cushions around, the code wouldn't work. Can you think of a way to write some code that would work for all kinds of different obstacle courses?

USE "IF"

You could try to use the command "If." Code such as "If" is known as a **conditional** statement. The code asks if a **condition** exists. If the condition does exist, then the code tells the computer to do something.

CODING TIPS

"If" commands are very useful. They mean that your computer can now make simple decisions. Instead of blindly doing something, it tests to see if it can.

How would "If" help with the cushions?

Using "If" in the code would tell the robot to ask "If a cushion is in front of you, step to the right."

Play this "If" racing game with a friend. Cut some card stock into 8 squares. On four cards, draw a shape. On the other four cards, draw a color. Put the cards into a bag. Take turns pulling a card from the bag. For your first card, you can choose which square on the board you start from. For example, if you get a circle, you can choose to start from the red or blue circle. Then "If" your card's color or shape is next to your counter's square in any direction, you may move there. Put the card back after each turn and shake the bag to shuffle it.

Make these cards

Finish

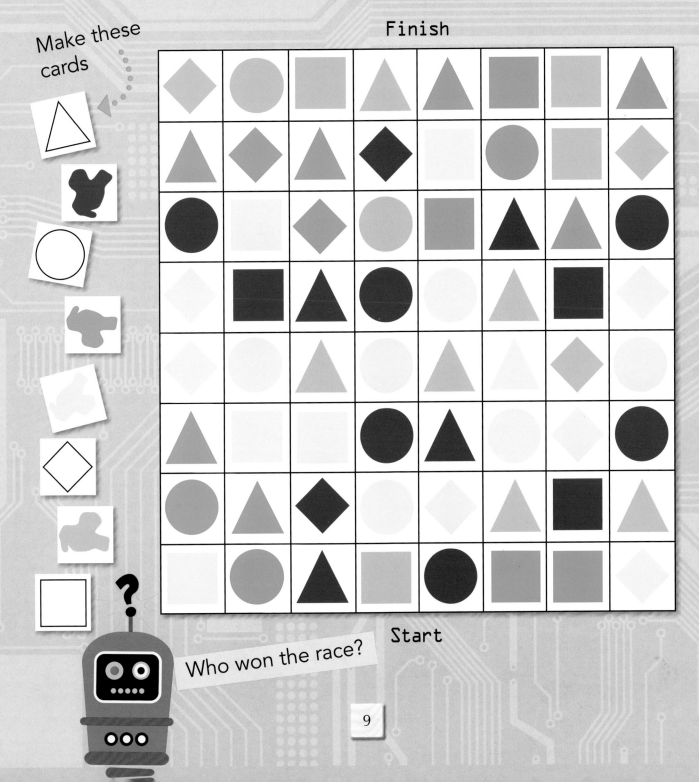

Start

Who won the race?

What Do "If" and "Else" Do?

There are some other really useful conditional statements that make coding really smart. Coders will often use "If" with the conditional statement "Else." If we were back at our cushion obstacle course, we could ask the robot "If there is a cushion in front of you, then step to the right, Else move forward."

THE IF GAME

You could try this game with some friends. It's a little like "Simon Says." Choose one of you to be the programmer. They stand in front of the "computers" and give them instructions. They need to give their computers something to do for the condition, "If." For example:

"If I raise both arms, then jog in place."

In this example, if the programmer raises their arms, the "computers" must all jog in place. When the programmer puts their arms down, they should stop.

In addition to "If," coders use the conditional statement "Else." Imagine the "If" game became the "If, Else" game. The programmer could say, "If I raise both arms, then jog in place, Else you sit down." This condition adds another instruction for the computers to follow. Using conditional statements means that instead of just following instructions, your computer can start to make decisions.

GET Programming

Using the game board on page 9, you could try a different game using If, Else conditions. Now, "If" the color or shape on the card that you draw out of the bag is in front of you, then step forward, "Else" move one space backward.

CODING TIPS

The "If" part of a condition tells your program to run a block of code as long as the condition it asks is true. The statement "If I raise both arms" prompts the computer to ask "Are both arms raised?" True? — then jog. False? — do nothing. The "Else" condition gives another possible action to your code. It answers the question "Should I do something if the answer is false?" Yes — sit down.

Can computers really make decisions?

No, a computer just does what it is told. Your code tells the computer what questions to ask and how to respond. The computer can't make decisions by itself.

All About Loops

Sometimes simple coding can get a little **repetitive**. Because you have to tell a computer to do everything very precisely, if you asked your computer-powered robot to hop, he would hop once. What would you do if you wanted him to hop some more times? You could just repeat the instruction, "Hop," "Hop," "Hop," "Hop" and so on. Or, you could use a **loop**.

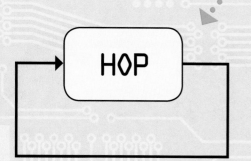

A loop will help get your robot to keep hopping without you having to tell it to every few seconds. There are several different kinds of loops depending on how long you want your robot to hop for and why you would want him to stop.

How do loops work?

A loop will ask the computer to keep repeating the same thing you told it to do until it meets a condition which tells it to stop.

TYPES OF LOOPS

Loops let you repeat a set of instructions. Different types of loops work in different ways. The main difference is when they stop looping. How they stop is called their terminating condition. Terminating just means stopping.

A For Loop

This loop tells the computer to do something a certain number of times. You could tell the robot to "Jump Six Times" using a For Loop.

An Endless Loop

This loop never stops because it has no terminating condition, the condition can never be met, or it has a condition that causes the loop to repeat! The poor robot would hop and hop forever.

A While Loop

This loop tells the computer to keep doing something based on a condition. It's like an "If" that keeps repeating. You could program the robot with the code "While I have my hands in the air, Hop."

GET Programming

Can you work out which type of loop you might need for the tasks below? Would you need a "For" Loop, a "While" Loop, or an "Endless" Loop?

a) Make a doorbell ring just while the button is being pressed.

b) Code an alarm clock to beep 10 times at a set time.

c) Tell your computer's clock to start counting the seconds.

d) Turn on a light for one minute.

Answers are on page 32

Words and Logic

C
A
T

Computers can be coded to **process** words that we type on a keyboard. They may not understand the words that we are typing. However, their code allows them to follow the commands that we type as if they do understand. Computers can even use logic to work out if we have made a mistake while we type.

Have you ever typed a word into a **search engine** and spelled it a bit wrong? Usually, the search engine can work out what you meant to type and find what you were searching for anyhow. That's clever!

When we read a sentence with words we don't understand, we can use the words in the sentence we do know to guess what the others mean. Computers can't understand words like we can, but they can quickly unscramble scrambled-up words into words that they know.

SCRAMBLED WORDS

See if you can work out what this scrambled sentence says using your own logic.

"It deosn't mttaer waht oredr ltteers in a wrod are. The olny iprmoatnt tihng is the frist and lsat ltteer are in the rghit pclae!"

Answers are on page 32

How do computers process what we type? Coders use a method known as ASCII. Each letter and symbol is given an ASCII number. That number is then translated into a 7-**bit** binary number, made up of 0s and 1s. 127 possible keyboard characters can be given a code in this way. ASCII stands for American Standard Code for Information Interchange. You can see why they shortened it!

Why do we have to turn the ASCII number into 0s and 1s?

Because computers understand binary!

GET Programming

Look at the ASCII numbers chart on the right. Can you decode these words below from their ASCII numbers?

a) 72, 69, 76, 76, 79

b) 82, 79, 66, 79, 84

c) 66, 73, 78, 65, 82, 89

d) 65, 83, 67, 73, 73

Answers are on page 32

65=A	78=N
66=B	79=O
67=C	80=P
68=D	81=Q
69=E	82=R
70=F	83=S
71=G	84=T
72=H	85=U
73=I	86=V
74=J	87=W
75=K	88=X
76=L	89=Y
77=M	90=Z

Boolean Logic

Computers use a special type of logic known as **binary logic**. Binary logic uses the computer's two electrical states — on or off — to tell the computer to do things. Any data a computer uses has to be converted into binary. The binary number system uses two numbers, 0 and 1. 0 = off, and 1 = on.

GEORGE BOOLE

In the 1800s, George Boole developed a simple system of logic. He didn't develop it for computers to use, because they didn't exist then. Early computer developers realized Boole's system was perfect for computers to use because it simply asked whether something was true or false. In Boolean logic, 0 = False, and 1 = True.

Does Boolean Logic just test if something is true or not?

No, it can do more, by adding "And," "Or," and "Not." It can work out problems such as "If this is true, and that is not true, then do this."

GET Programming

Try this new game using Boolean logic. Add three more cards, AND, OR, and NOT. Put the cards into a new bag. Place your counter by a shape on the start line. In turn, pick a card from the Boolean bag. If you pick a NOT card take one card from the colors and shapes bag. If you get AND or OR, take two cards.

Now test the symbols around your counter against the cards you have drawn to see if you can move. IF Red AND Triangle (move to that square), or IF Green OR Yellow (move to that square) or If NOT square (move to that square).

Make these new cards

Finish

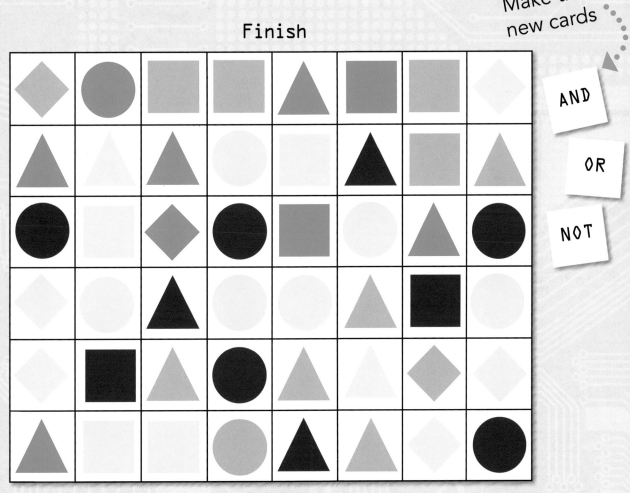

Start

AND

OR

NOT

Switch Statements

Sometimes your code needs to choose to do something based on a number of possible outcomes. Computers use switch statements.

The switch statement accepts a **value**. It then checks "cases" to find that value. When the condition is met and it finds the value, the block of code is run. The rest of the switch statement can be skipped once the code has found what it was looking for.

DECIDING WHAT TO WEAR

Imagine you are standing in front of your closet, deciding which T-shirt to wear. You could look at each T-shirt in turn and ask "Do I want to wear this T-shirt?" More likely, you look at all your T-shirts at once, and pick the one that screams "Wear me!"

Maybe today you really feel like wearing a white T-shirt. Create a switch statement which asks:
"Is the T-shirt white?"
If the answer is "Yes," wear this T-shirt.
If the answer is no, keep looking.
If no white T-shirts are found, you might want to add a **default**, so you don't end up with no T-shirt at all. The default might be:
Wear a blue T-shirt

18

GET Programming

Read the switch statement below. Can you guess what the result of our switch statement would be? The time is 4 p.m.

Our switch statement asks:

case 1: 9 a.m.	say "Good morning"
case 2: 4 p.m.	say "Good afternoon"
case 3: 7 p.m.	say "Good evening"
case 4: 11 p.m.	say "Good night"
default:	say "Hello"

Which of these would be our result?

a) `Good morning`

c) `Hello`

b) `Good afternoon`

d) `Good night`

Answers are on page 32

DICE RACE GAME

This switch statement game chooses an action based on a dice roll. See who can get across a room the fastest playing this dice game.

Switch
    case 1: Take 1 step
    case 2: Turn right
    case 3: Turn left
    case 4: Take 2 steps
    case 5: Step backwards
    case 6: Jump

Why does this game not have a default?

You only need a default if all the possibilities aren't covered. A dice only has 6 possible numbers.

More About Loops

We have already talked a little about different kinds of loops. The While loop is really useful when writing code. The advantage of a While loop is that it will repeat a task as often as necessary to achieve its goal. While a condition is being met, the While loop will keep doing what it is doing. There is also a similar loop we can use, known as an **Until loop**.

While and Until loops have a lot in common, but there is an important difference. A While loop asks the question at the start of the code, and an Until loop asks the question at the end. Can you see the difference between running these two bits of code?

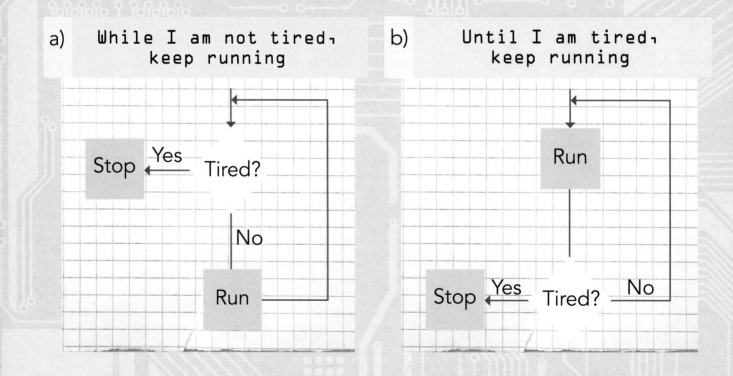

a) **While I am not tired, keep running**

b) **Until I am tired, keep running**

CODING TIPS

With an Until loop, the code runs one time and then tests to see if the robot is tired. You would not want to use an Until loop if it was dangerous to run the loop. If the condition was true, and the robot was tired, it might hurt him to run.

Run until you are tired!

GET Programming

There are times when you must use an Until loop rather than a While loop. Which of these situations would need an Until loop, where you run the code before you test for your condition?

a. You want to keep juggling two balls until you drop one.

b. While your car has gas, keep driving.

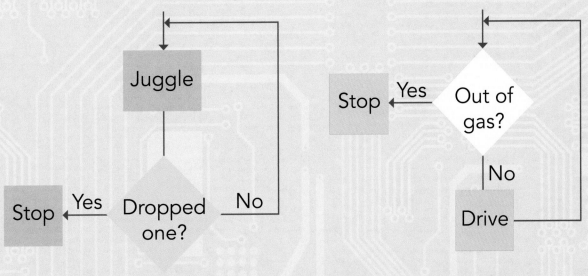

Juggle

Stop ← Yes — Dropped one? — No

Stop ← Yes — Out of gas?

No

Drive

Answers are on page 32

Call the Operators

Operators are math symbols that we use in our code, such as + (plus), - (minus) , < (less than), and > (greater than). They work pretty much the same as they work in math. An operator tells the computer what to do with any number values.

I often get the < and > symbol confused!

Just think of it like a hungry alligator's mouth. The alligator wants to eat the biggest number, so his mouth faces that way.

15 ⟩ 10

greater than >

7 ⟨ 9

less than <

equal to =

Which operator should you use between these numbers, <, >, or =?
a) 6, 8
b) 4, 4
c) 12, 6

Answers are on page 32

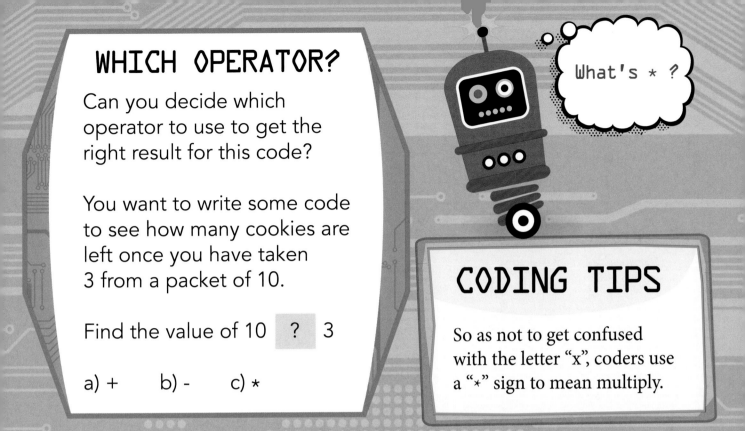

WHICH OPERATOR?

Can you decide which operator to use to get the right result for this code?

You want to write some code to see how many cookies are left once you have taken 3 from a packet of 10.

Find the value of 10 ? 3

a) +   b) -   c) *

What's * ?

CODING TIPS

So as not to get confused with the letter "x", coders use a "*" sign to mean multiply.

GET Programming

Try playing this "Greater Than/Less Than" game with a friend. You will need a pack of playing cards.

Take out the Jacks, Queens, and Kings and then shuffle the remaining cards. You start the game by someone picking two cards from the pile. They lay the two cards down and add their card's values to find the sum. The next player has their turn. The player with the greatest sum takes all four cards. Whoever has the most cards at the end is the winner.

Now play the game again and turn it on its head. This time, find the difference between the two cards. The lowest number wins and gives their cards to the loser. The player with the fewest cards at the end is the winner.

A Logical Order

Sometimes it really matters what order you do things in. In coding, the order things are done in is called **precedence**. You've seen that when you write instructions, the order is important. It is also important when working with values.

You may have seen that order can matter in math. If you have three numbers and an add symbol, it doesn't matter what order you do them in. 3+2+4 equals the same as 2+4+3.

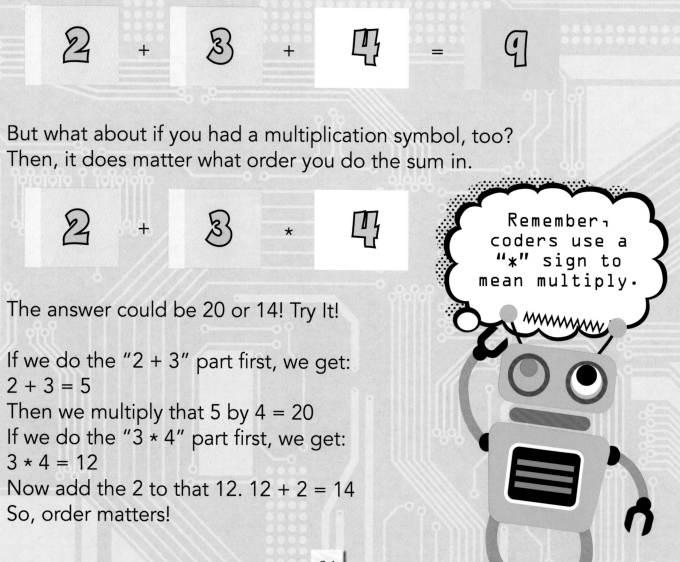

2 + 3 + 4 = 9

But what about if you had a multiplication symbol, too? Then, it does matter what order you do the sum in.

2 + 3 * 4

Remember, coders use a "*" sign to mean multiply.

The answer could be 20 or 14! Try It!

If we do the "2 + 3" part first, we get:
2 + 3 = 5
Then we multiply that 5 by 4 = 20
If we do the "3 * 4" part first, we get:
3 * 4 = 12
Now add the 2 to that 12. 12 + 2 = 14
So, order matters!

CODING TIPS

Coders have developed some simple rules about what order to do things in, so they never get the wrong answer. They will usually do any multiplication and division first. Also, anything put in brackets ( ) tells us that needs to be worked out first. The equation on page 24 could have been written 2 + (3 * 4).

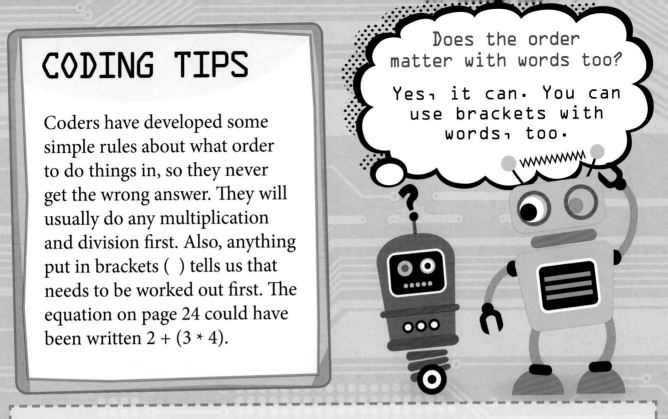

Does the order matter with words too?

Yes, it can. You can use brackets with words, too.

GET Programming

Imagine you're ordering a sandwich. You'd like a peanut butter and jelly sandwich, or a ham sandwich. You write some code to check you have the ingredients. Usually code works from left to right, just the same as we read words. So your code might ask:

Ham or Peanut Butter and Jelly

As it is, the code will check if you have ham or peanut butter. You do have ham, but no peanut butter. Then the code will check if you have jelly. Great news, we have jelly. So, you get a ham and jelly sandwich! Yuck!

Could brackets help get the right sandwich?
Ham or (Peanut Butter and Jelly)

The code checks if you have peanut butter and jelly first. If you don't have both, and you have ham, you just get ham. Phew!

Logical Decisions

Creating code can get complicated. Writing down your code helps you plan what you want it to do, and in what order. An algorithm can be made into a diagram known as a **flowchart**. The flowchart shows all the steps that you need to take and decisions that you might need to make.

FLOWCHARTS

Flowcharts are simple diagrams. Each step is represented by a different shaped symbol. A short description of the step is written in each symbol. The symbols are linked together with arrows that show the direction the process should follow. Below is a simple flowchart. Try making a flowchart of something you do every day.

Start/End

Decision

Process

Input/Output

direction

Packing Your Bag for School

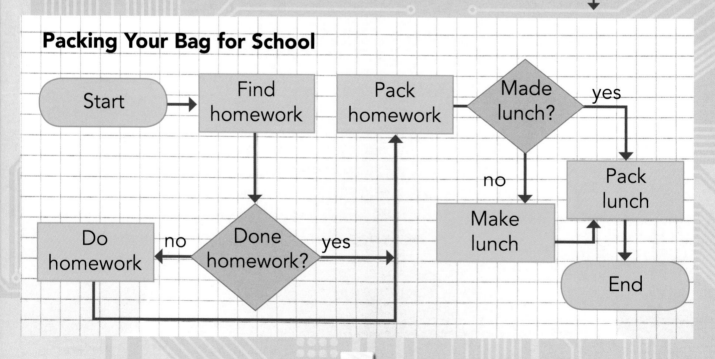

Start → Find homework → Pack homework → Made lunch? — yes → Pack lunch → End

Made lunch? — no → Make lunch → Pack lunch

Find homework → Done homework? — no → Do homework

Done homework? — yes → Pack homework

GET Programming

Decisions allow more than one path through a program. Using If and Else gives two possible choices. You can draw your If/Else code in a flowchart to check it will work.

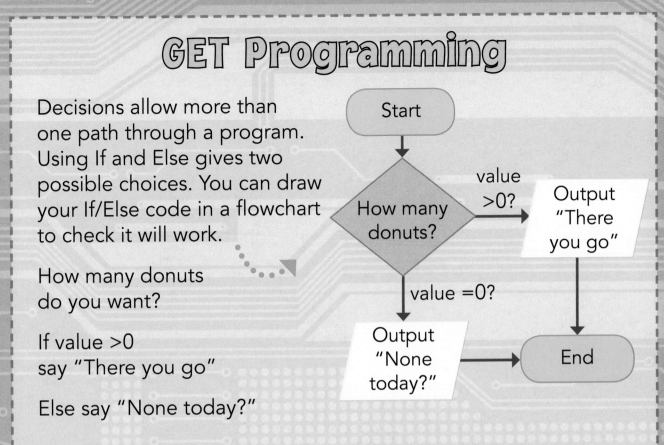

How many donuts do you want?

If value >0
say "There you go"

Else say "None today?"

For more than two choices, you could add an Else If statement.

If value =2 say "Enjoy them both"
Else If value >0 say "There you go"
Else say "None today?"

Does the order matter when you use Else If?

Yes. The code stops checking once it finds a "yes" answer. So say the >0 came before the =2, the program would never look beyond >0, and never say "Enjoy them both."

Can You Pass the Test?

1. What number system does a computer use?
   a) unary b) denary c) binary

2. What is an algorithm?
   a) a set of instructions for a computer
   b) a robot
   c) music that is played on a computer

3. Which of these is a conditional statement in computing?
   a) But b) If c) Old

4. What sort of loop would you use if you wanted your loop to never stop looping?
   a) a For Loop b) an Endless Loop

5. Look at the ASCII table on page 15. Can you work out what this sentence says? The underscore _ is a space.
   71, 79, 79, 68 _ 74, 79, 66 _
   87, 69, 76, 76 _ 68, 79, 78, 69

6. What did George Boole invent?
   a) the hairdryer
   b) Boolean Logic c) robots

I think I got some right! Did you?

7. Which symbol do you need between these pairs of numbers, < or >?
   a) 14, 7   b) 3, 5   c) 12, 128

8. If you see brackets around parts of a math equation in code, such as 3 + (7 * 3), what does that mean?
   a) do the part of the equation in brackets first
   b) do the part of the equation in brackets last

9. What does "precedence" mean?
   a) the order that things are done in coding
   b) something you get on your birthday
   c) the most important person in the USA

10. What could you draw to help you plan out your code?
    a) a picture of a computer
    b) a flowchart
    c) a doodle of your brain

Turn this page upside down to see the answers.

Quiz Answers

1. c) binary; 2. a) a set of instructions for a computer; 3. b) If; 4. b) an Endless Loop; 5. GOOD JOB WELL DONE; 6. b) Boolean Logic; 7. a) >; b) <; c) <; 8. a) do the part of the equation in brackets first; 9. a) the order that things are done in coding; 10. b) a flowchart

Glossary

algorithm A step-by-step method for solving a problem.

ASCII A code for representing characters as numbers.

binary A system of numbers having two as its base.

binary logic Processing based on the binary numbering system.

bit A unit of computer information that represents the selection of one of two possible choices.

condition Something essential to the occurrence of something else.

conditional Depending on a condition.

default A selection to be made automatically when the user does not specify a choice.

Endless Loop A loop that never stops looping.

For Loop A loop that tells the computer to do something a certain number of times.

flowchart A graphic representation of a logic sequence.

logic Sound reasoning.

loop A series of computer instructions repeated until a requirement for ending is met.

operators A character that represents an action.

precedence The order in which certain operations need to be performed.

precise Very exact.

process To take in and organize for use in a variety of ways.

program Give step-by-step instructions that tell a computer to do something with data.

random Showing no clear plan, purpose, or pattern.

repetitive Something done over and over again.

search engine A website used to search data.

Until Loop A loop that tells the computer to keep doing something based on a condition at the end of the loop.

value A number or word assigned to an object.

While Loop A loop that tells the computer to keep doing something based on a condition at the start of the loop.

For More Information

BOOKS

Anniss, Matthew. *Understanding Programming and Logic (Infosearch: Understanding Computing)*. Mankato, MN: Raintree, 2016.

Woodcock, Jon. *Coding Games with Scratch*. DK Children, 2015.

For web resources related to the subject of this book, go to: **www.windmillbooks.com/weblinks** and select this book's title.

Index

Answers

page 5: a) 1, b) 2, c) 3; page 6: 1, 2, 3, 5, 4; page 13: a) While Loop, b) For Loop, c) Endless Loop, d) For Loop; page 14: It doesn't matter what order the letters in a word are. The only important thing is the first and last letters are in the right place!; page 15: a) HELLO, b) ROBOT, c) BINARY, d) ASCII; page 19: b) Good afternoon; page 21: a) because you can't run your car if it has no gas; page 22: a) <, b) =, c) >; page 23: b) -;